SUPER BOWL CHAMPIONS
BALTIMORE RAVENS

TIGHT END ED DICKSON

SUPER BOWL CHAMPIONS
BALTIMORE RAVENS

AARON FRISCH

CREATIVE
PAPERBACKS

Published by Creative Paperbacks
P.O. Box 227, Mankato, Minnesota 56002
Creative Paperbacks is an imprint of The Creative Company
www.thecreativecompany.us

Design and production by Blue Design
Art direction by Rita Marshall
Printed in the United States of America

Photographs by Getty Images (Simon Bruty/Sports
Illustrated, TIMOTHY A. CLARY/AFP, G Flume, Otto Greule
Jr., Doug Kapustin/MCT, Ronald Martinez, Doug Pensinger,
Patrick Smith, Matt Sullivan, Gene Sweeney Jr./Baltimore
Sun/MCT, Travel Ink, Rob Tringali/SportsChrome, Greg
Trott, Dilip Vishwanat, Nick Wass)

Library of Congress Cataloging-in-Publication Data
Frisch, Aaron.
Baltimore Ravens / Aaron Frisch.
p. cm. — (Super bowl champions)
Includes index.
Summary: An elementary look at the Baltimore Ravens
professional football team, including its formation in 1996,
most memorable players, Super Bowl championships, and
stars of today.
ISBN 978-1-60818-372-2 (hardcover)
ISBN 978-0-89812-951-9 (pbk)
1. Baltimore Ravens (Football team)—History—Juvenile
literature. I. Title.

GV956.B3F74 2013
796.332'64097526—dc23   2013009757

First Edition
9 8 7 6 5 4 3 2 1

RUNNING BACK WILLIS McGAHEE

JONATHAN OGDEN / 1996–2007

Jonathan was a giant offensive tackle (6-foot-9 and 340 pounds!) who blocked other teams' biggest players.

TABLE OF CONTENTS

BRIAN BILLICK / 1999–2007

Brian was Baltimore's second coach. He was the first Ravens coach to win a Super Bowl.

BROWNS BECOME RAVENS

In 1995, the Cleveland Browns football team moved to Baltimore, Maryland. It needed a new name and uniforms. The Baltimore Ravens were born!

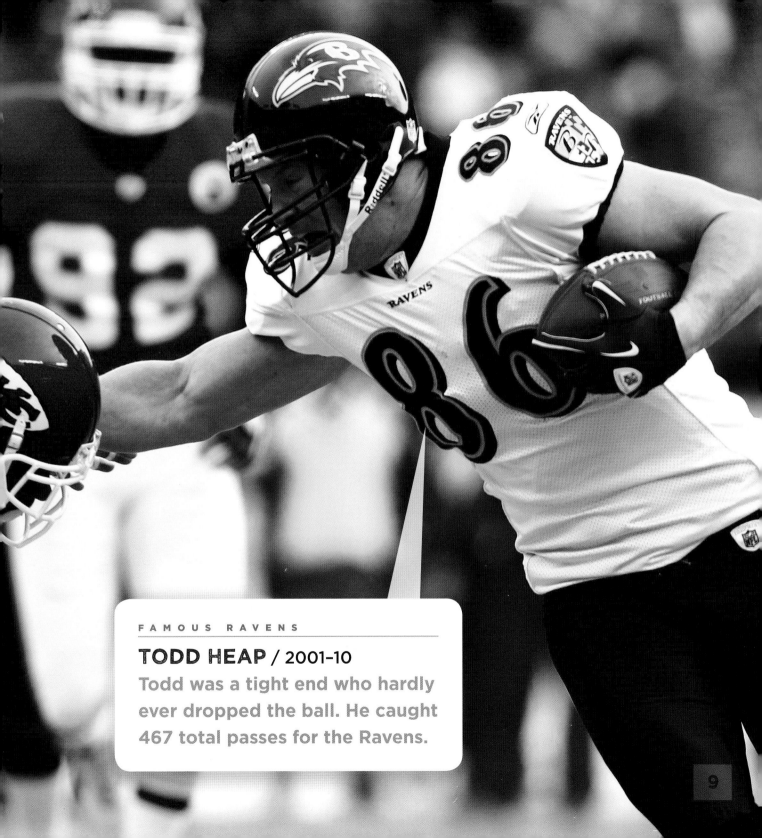

TODD HEAP / 2001–10

Todd was a tight end who hardly
ever dropped the ball. He caught
467 total passes for the Ravens.

A BALTIMORE WRITER

A writer named Edgar Allan Poe used to live in Baltimore. He wrote a famous poem called "The Raven." That's how Baltimore's football team was named.

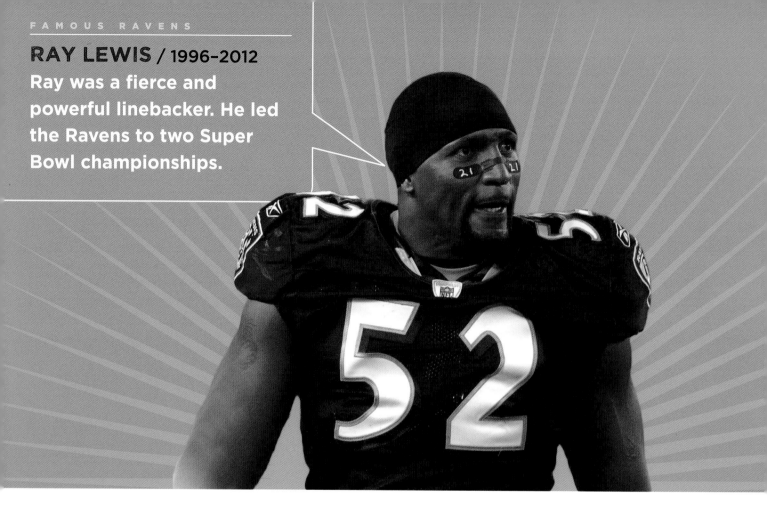

RAY LEWIS / 1996–2012
Ray was a fierce and powerful linebacker. He led the Ravens to two Super Bowl championships.

ONE TOUGH DEFENSE

Baltimore's team is known for its hard-hitting defense. Some people think the 2000 Ravens team had the best defense in National Football League (NFL) history!

2007 RAVENS DEFENSE

13

JAMAL LEWIS

THE RAVENS' STORY

The Ravens started playing in 1996. They lost a lot of games at first. But they added great defensive players and a powerful running back named Jamal Lewis.

In 2000, the Ravens had a super-tough defense. They got to Super Bowl XXXV (35). Then they beat the New York Giants 34–7 to become world champs!

QUARTERBACK
VINNY TESTAVERDE

TERRELL SUGGS

The Ravens were a **contender** most seasons after that. Fans cheered for new stars like linebacker Terrell Suggs. Terrell **sacked** many quarterbacks.

ED REED

2002–12

Ed was a fast safety. He was great at making **interceptions** and then scoring touchdowns.

17

ANQUAN BOLDIN

SOUND IT OUT
ANQUAN: *AN-kwahn*

SOUND IT OUT

HARBAUGH: *HAR-bah*

JOHN HARBAUGH

John Harbaugh became the Ravens' coach in 2008. He was good at getting players fired up. The Ravens won at least one **playoff** game in each of his first four years.

With players like wide receiver Anquan Boldin, the Ravens were hard to beat. In 2008 and 2011, they came just one win short of the Super Bowl.

FAMOUS RAVENS

JOE FLACCO / 2008–present
Joe was a quarterback with a strong throwing arm. He was a calm leader for the offense, too.

SOUND IT OUT
FLACCO: *FLAK-oh*

By 2013, Ray Rice helped keep the Ravens exciting. Ray was a short but strong running back. He and his teammates flew to their second championship in February and hoped to get another soon!

RAY RICE

FACTS FILE

CONFERENCE/DIVISION:
American Football Conference, North Division

TEAM COLORS:
Purple and black

HOME STADIUM:
M&T Bank Stadium

SUPER BOWL VICTORIES:
XXXV, January 28, 2001 34–7 over New York Giants
XLVII, February 3, 2013 34–31 over San Francisco 49ers

NFL WEBSITE FOR KIDS:
http://nflrush.com

GLOSSARY

contender — a talented team that has a good chance of winning a championship

interceptions — plays in which a defensive player catches a pass thrown by the other team

playoff — one of the games that the best teams play after a season to see who the champion will be

sacked — tackled a quarterback who was trying to throw a pass

INDEX